Our deepest appreciation to those who helped bring this book to life:

Jae Park for sharing his resources and for believing in us, and this book.
The 'thought leaders' that inspired the content – James Wedmore,
Jim Fortin, Dr. Shannon Irvine and Dr. Caroline Leaf

The team at yemmibooks for doing such a beautiful job of turning our words
and pictures into something solid we can hold in our hands and treasure!

Most of all – to all our family and friends that are so supportive and expressed such
love and delight over this book. We are so thankful for all of you!

I'M THE THINKER OF MY THOUGHTS

First published in Korea by yemmibooks in 2020
ISBN 979-11-89877-22-4
Text copyright © 2019 Noella Reeder All rights reserved
Illustrations copyright © A.G. Reeder 2019

Hasung Plaza #601, 1568, Jungang-ro. Ilsanseo-gu, Goyang-si. Gyeonggi-do, Republic of Korea
yemmibooks@naver.com
Printed in Korea

At home my parents do things to take care of me

At school my teacher helps me become as smart as I can be

But only I can help myself on the inside

I control my thoughts and the things I decide

My mind is like my house where I eat, sleep and stay

And my thoughts are like the friends I have over to play

Some thoughts are like good friends that make me feel nice

Others are like people I won't have over twice

They can make me feel mad, bad, and sad
And send me crying to my Mom or Dad

I can choose my thoughts like I can choose a friend
So, I choose ones that treat me well, faithful till the end

**When thoughts show up that I didn't invite
and start being mean and picking a fight**

I can tell them to leave and not come back

And if they knock on my door, I won't open it a crack!

I'll tell them that they have to stay out
Because I have better things to think about!

I'm the thinker of my thoughts
They don't rule me, they're like my robots

**My thoughts do what I tell them to do
I can choose to have many...**

or only a few.

My thoughts are there to serve me
I want ones that make me happy

If a thought doesn't put a smile on my face
I will just put another one in its place!

Every thought in my head affects how I feel
They don't seem like much, but their power is real!

Each feeling I feel leads to an action
Which can bring me sadness...

...or satisfaction!

I want what I do to make me feel good

I'll pick thoughts that help me do things I should

**I'm the one who decides what thoughts stay in my mind
I'm going to collect the best ones I can find!**

I want to live in peace and harmony
So, I choose thoughts that help build the best me!

Author's tips for reading this book with children:

Thank you for choosing this book. I hope it will promote a lifetime of constructive thinking that can lead to mental and emotional health, as well as success and personal growth. I encourage you to ask questions after reading to reinforce the concepts. Help them understand the connection between their thoughts, which create feelings, that lead to actions. Discuss the difference between helpful and unhelpful thoughts and try to come up with some ideas of good thoughts that can replace harmful ones. It's also important to remind children (and ourselves!) that everyone, even the nicest people, have 'bad' thoughts sometimes, but it's what we do with them that matters!

I hope you'll have a lifetime full of awesome thoughts!

Noella Reeder

Noella Reeder - Author

Noella Reeder is a mom and grandma whose superpower is writing poetry. She loves to take important concepts and put them into poems and songs to help people remember them. She doesn't have a PhD, but has a passion for learning about self-improvement, and understands that all true change must first start in the mind. Her favorite thoughts are all the things she's thankful for, like her family and friends!

A.G. Reeder - Illustrator

A.G. Reeder has been drawing since he was old enough to hold a pencil. He loves dogs and dreams of having his own one day, which is why the boy in the story has such an adorable pup! Illustrating this book was therapeutic to him, because it's based on concepts used in therapy for trauma and other mental health issues like anxiety. It is called CBT, short for Cognitive Behavioral Therapy, which he has found very helpful in his own healing journey.